英訳付き
包む折り紙

Origami Booklet

Fold and Give : Boxes and Pouches

監修／小林一夫

Editorial Supervisor
Kazuo Kobayashi

はじめに

包んで贈る、慎みの心

　日本の折り紙のルーツといわれるのが、今から六百年ほど前の武家社会に生まれた「折形（おりかた）」という礼法です。武家の間では、冠婚葬祭や日常的な贈り物をするときも、必ず和紙で包んで届けました。その包み方や折り方を作法として定めたのが「折形」で、儀礼折り紙とも呼ばれます。

　この「折形」をもとに、工夫と遊び心を加えて新たな形をつくりだし、鶴をはじめ、動植物や生活道具に見立てて楽しむようになったのが、いま私たちが親しんでいる折り紙（遊戯折り紙）のはじまりと考えられています。

　この本では、「折形」から派生した包みや入れものとなる折り紙や、「たとう」と呼ばれる伝承折り紙を中心に紹介しています。美しく折り、包むという習慣には、相手への謙虚さや優しい心づかいが表れています。「包む心」は「日本人の慎（つつし）みの心」でもあるのです。美しい伝統文様の江戸千代紙とともに、日本の心を折り紙で楽しんでください。海外へのおみやげとしても喜ばれると思います。

国際おりがみ協会理事長　小林一夫

Introduction

Wrap and Give: The Spirit of Modesty

The etiquette of *orikata*, which is said to be the root of Japanese origami, arose in the samurai class about 600 years ago. When samurai families gave gifts on everyday occasions and at special events such as weddings, they always wrapped them in *washi* paper first. *Orikata*, also called "formal origami," are polite ways to wrap with paper.

New shapes were created based on these *orikata* through innovation and a sense of fun. People soon began to enjoy creating models, such as the paper crane, that resembled plants, animals and the things of daily life. This is thought to be the origin of the recreational origami we are familiar with today.

In this book, we mainly introduce origami wrappings and pouches derived from *orikata* and traditional origami models called *tatos*. Humility and a kind regard for others are expressed by the Japanese customs of beautifully folding paper and wrapping gifts.

This spirit of wrapping is the Japanese spirit of modesty. Please enjoy the spirit of Japan through both origami and the beautiful traditional patterns of *edo chiyogami*. This book also makes a perfect gift for friends around the world.

K. Kobayashi

Kazuo Kobayashi
The Chairman of the International Origami Association

Contents

八角たとう
Octagonal Tato

六角つなぎ Rokkaku-tsunagi

折据
Orisue

博多縞 Hakata-jima

紅入れ
Beni Pouch

槍梅 Yari-ume

バラ
Rose

匹田鹿の子 Hitta-kanoko

鶴のたとう
Crane Tato

唐松 Karamatsu

鶴の入れもの
Crane Mini Box

花丸紋重ね Hana Marumon-kasane

折り方 How to Fold the Models

日本の包む文化と折る文化

　日本の折り紙が広く親しまれ、発展してきた背景には、日本の和紙の文化、包む文化がありました。白い和紙で物を包むという習慣は平安時代に始まり、室町時代（1336年-1573年）には、贈答品やお金を贈るときの包み方を定めた「折形」が上級武士の社会に広まっていきました。「折形」は、扇包み、帯包み、香包みなど、品物の種類によって包み方や紙の折り方が定められ、受け取る側はその包みの形を見るだけで、中身が何であるかを知ることができました。和紙で美しく「包む」ことで、贈る側の誠意と謙譲の心を表わし、また装飾的な折り方で品物を効果的に見せながら、中身を保護するという役割もありました。

　現在でも日本では、贈り物でもお祝いのお金でもけっしてむき出しのまま渡したりせず、紙や布で包むという習慣があり、簡略化された熨斗袋や水引きにも「折形」の名残が見られます。また、贈り物を受け取って、相手の目の前ですぐ包みを開けたり、嬉しさからすぐ包装紙を破って中身を確認するという行為が日本人になじまないのは、こうした贈る人の心を伝える「包む文化」がまだ日本人の心に残っているせいではないでしょうか。

　上質の和紙は高価なものでしたが、江戸時代中頃から安価な和紙が量産されるようになり、下級武士や庶民の間でも和紙が日常で使われるようになりました。「折形」もまた格式の高い礼法としてだけでなく、人々の生活の中で利用されるようになり、さまざまな流派や様式が生まれました。やがて「折形」から、折り鶴や帆掛け舟などの独立した形を折って楽しむ「遊戯折り紙」が生まれ、いまや世界的に普及する日本の折り紙文化のもとになったのです。

Japan's Culture of Wrapping and Folding

Behind the development of the Japanese origami that is known to many people today is Japan's cultures of *washi* (traditional paper) and wrapping.

The custom of wrapping things in white *washi* paper began in the Heian era (794 to 1185), and in the Muromachi era (1336 to 1573) rules of etiquette called *orikata*, which described how to wrap gifts and money, became popular among upper class samurai. Rules for using *orikata* such as the fan wrap, obi wrap and incense wrap depended on the content of the gift, and the receiver could tell the content of a gift just by seeing how it was wrapped. By beautifully wrapping with *washi*, the giver could express sincerity and respect, and decorative ways of folding served the role of effectively conveying what was in a package while protecting its content.

Even today, Japanese custom dictates that presents and gifts of money never be given without first wrapping in paper or cloth, and remnants of *orikata* may be seen in simplified *noshi* decorations and *mizuhiki* (red and white string decorations) that are still used. When Japanese people receive gifts, they are not comfortable with quickly unwrapping them in front of the giver, and do not quickly rip the wrapping paper in glee to check what is inside. Perhaps this is due to the fact that the old "wrapping culture," which conveys the feelings of the giver, still remains in our hearts.

Although high quality *washi* was expensive, affordable *washi* came to be produced in high volume from about the middle of the Edo era (1603 to 1867), allowing lower-class samurai and regular people to use it every day. *Orikata* were no longer just high-status rules of etiquette, but were used by many people for daily activities, giving rise to a variety of teaching styles and designs. Eventually, individual models such as the paper crane and boat with sails were created from *orikata* for fun, and "recreational origami" came to be. This is where the culture of Japanese origami that has become so popular around the world began.

「折形」とは 「たとう」とは

　「折形」は、記録によれば約六百年前には「包みの折方」という名でその様式が定められていたそうです。以後、折形は武家の礼法の一つとして、秘伝あるいは口伝によって受け継がれていき、また見本となる「雛形」が和紙で一式作られ、代々の当主に伝えられていきました。江戸・明治時代を通して一般社会にも広まり、明治中期から昭和初期頃までは、身に付けるべき礼儀作法の一つとして、高等女学校や女子師範学校の作法教科書にも折形の図が掲載されていました。折形にはさまざまな約束ごとがあり、まず物があってその形に合わせて紙を折り込むことで、物の上下や左右を間違えることもありません。結婚式の祝儀袋に紙幣を入れ忘れるなどという失態も起こりえないのです。贈り先の格式に応じて使う和紙の種類にもランクがありました。「雄蝶・雌蝶」など慶事の装飾用の折形もあります。また「切る」ことは慶事には禁忌なのではさみや糊も一切使わず、「袋」ではなく「包み」なので物を封じ込めません。物を完全に包み込まず、一部が必ず見えるように包むという約束もあります。こうした伝統文化が現在ほとんど伝えられていないのは残念なことです。

　「たとう」とは「畳み紙」が変化した言葉で、「たとうがみ」ともいいます。一般には着物や結髪の道具を入れる厚手の和紙（渋や漆を塗って折り目をつけたもの）をたとうといいますが、たたんで懐に入れておく懐紙（ふところがみ。詩歌を書きつけたり、お茶や食事の席で菓子をとったり、器をぬぐったりするのにも使われる）のこともさします。「たたむ」とは普通「着物をたたむ、風呂敷をたたむ」のように元の形に戻せることをいい、折り紙では、一般に、紙を折りたたんで中が閉じ、開くこともできるものを「たとう」と呼び、たたまれた状態が花のように見えるものを「花たとう」と呼んでいます。

About Orikata and Tatos

According to records, the designs of *orikata* were created about 600 years ago and called "ways to fold for wrapping." After that, *orikata* were passed down as rules of etiquette of the samurai class, through families and by word of mouth. *Hinagata* books of *orikata* samples were also created from *washi*, and handed down to the head of the family from generation to generation. In the Edo era (1603 to 1867) and Meiji era (1868 to 1912) *orikata* became popular in common society. From the middle of the Meiji era to the start of the Showa era (1926 to 1989), *orikata* instructions were included in girls' high school and women's teaching school etiquette textbooks as manners that should be learned.

There are a number of conventions for *orikata*, the first of which is that the paper be folded to fit the shape of the object. The top and bottom and left and right of the object must also be unmistakable. Due to these folding conventions, blunder such as forgetting to enclose bills when wrapping money for weddings become impossible. Types of *washi* paper were also ranked according to the status of the receiver. There are even ornamental *orikata* such as *ocho* (male) and *mecho* (female) butterflies for festive occasions such as weddings. In addition, because cutting is taboo on such occasions, scissors and paste are never used. As *orikata* are wrappings rather than bags, the objects are not closed in. Objects must also not be completely wrapped as a small part must always be visible. Unfortunately, the greater part of this traditional culture has been lost to most people today.

The word *tato* comes from the word *tatami-gami*, which may also be called *tato-gami*. In general, thick *washi* papers used to wrap kimonos or tools for setting hair (pre-creased paper coated with tannin or lacquer) were called *tatos*, but *tato* also referred to the *kaishi* (thin paper used for writing poems, picking up sweets when drinking tea or at dinner, wiping dishes and so on) that were folded up and kept in pockets. The Japanese word *tatamu* (fold) is usually used to talk about folding things that can be returned to their original shape, such as kimonos or *furoshiki* (square cloths used to carry things). In origami, paper that is folded such that the inside can be opened or closed is called a *tato*, and if it looks like a flower when folded up, it is called a *hana* (flower) *tato*.

この本の使い方
Using This Book

この本の千代紙を使って、
25種類の折り紙作品がつくれます。
また、それぞれの紙の説明によって
日本の伝統文様について知ることができます。

You can make 25 origami models with
the *chiyogami* paper found in this book.
You will also learn about traditional
Japanese patterns from the explanations
that accompany each paper.

折り紙にこころも
包んで贈りましょう
Wrap your heart up
with origami
and give it away!

1 つくりたい作品を選びます。
Choose a model you would like to make.

2 ミシン線に合わせて紙をカットします。
ミシン線にいちど折り目をつけてからカットするときれいに切り取ることができます。
Cut the paper along the perforated line.
In order to cut the paper neatly, first make a crease along the perforated line.

3 折り方の載っているページを開きます。　例) see page 66
Open to the "How to Fold" page for your model. See page 66 for an example.

4 折り図を見ながら番号順に折っていきます。
完成した作品は、見本の写真と同じ位置に図柄（文様）が見えるとは限りません。
Look at the diagrams and fold in order.
On your completed models, the patterns will not necessarily appear
in the same position as in the sample photos.

5 できあがったら、好きな場所に飾ったり、友だちにプレゼントしましょう。
After you have finished, you can display your creation anywhere you please
or give it to a friend as a present.

6 折り方がわかったら、ほかの紙でも折ってみましょう。好きな色や柄、
いろいろな大きさの紙でつくってみると、さらに折り紙の楽しさが広がります。
Once you have got the idea, try making the model with different kinds of paper.
You can enjoy making these origami models again and again using different
sized papers of your favorite colors and designs.

この本で使う記号の意味
The Symbols Used in This Book

線の種類や矢印など、この本で使う記号の説明をします。
折り図を見るときに必要になるので記号の意味を覚えましょう。

Here we will explain the symbols used in this book, including the different folding lines and arrow marks. These symbols will help you understand the diagrams, so please remember them.

谷折り Valley fold (dashed line)

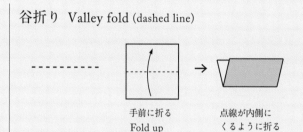

手前に折る
Fold up

点線が内側に
くるように折る

山折り Mountain fold (dashed-dotted line)

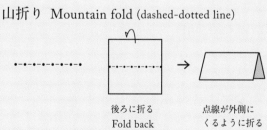

後ろに折る
Fold back

点線が外側に
くるように折る

折りすじをつける Make a crease (fold and unfold)

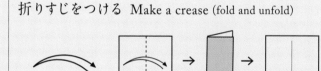

いちど折って線をつけたあと、紙をもどす

矢印の方向に折る Fold in the direction of the arrows

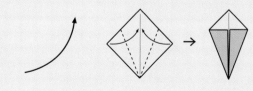

The Symbols Used in This Book

紙の向きを変える Rotate

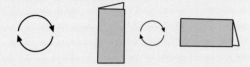

はさみを使う Use scissors

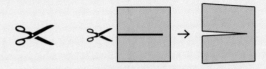

太線にそってはさみで切る
Cut along the thick line.

うらがえす Turn over

上下の位置は変えない
Do not change the orientation of the top and bottom.

紙のあいだを開く Insert fingers and open

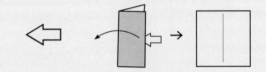

図を拡大する Enlargement

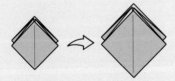

同じ幅・同じ角度 Same width, same angle

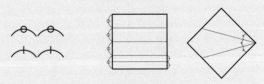

四角たとう
Square Tato

「たとう」は着物などを包む、畳紙<ruby>畳紙<rt>たたみがみ</rt></ruby>からきた言葉です。これは四角に折るたとうの一つで、紙を開いて中を見る楽しさもあります。

The word *tato* comes from *tato-gami* (folded paper used to wrap kimonos and so on). This is just one of many square shaped tatos. It is fun to open it and see what is inside.

see page 66

裾鶴

Suso-tsuru : Hem Crane

鶴は長寿や瑞祥の象徴とされ、めでた
い席にふさわしい吉祥文様です。これ
は着物の「裾模様」のように下から上
空に向けて飛び立つ鶴を描いた文様
で、花嫁衣装にも用いられました。

The crane is a symbol of long life
and happiness, making this lucky
pattern suitable for celebrations.
Here, cranes are taking flight from
the bottom up to the sky, as in a
kimono hem pattern. This pattern
was also used for bridal gowns.

<ruby>胡<rt>こ</rt>椒<rt>しょう</rt></ruby>包み
Pepper Wrapper

「折形」は贈答品の包み方を定め
た武家社会の礼法で、中身によっ
て折る形が決まっていました。こ
れは昔、貴重品だった胡椒を包ん
だ「折形」をアレンジしたもの。

Orikata were rules of etiquette
of the samurai class that
described how to wrap gifts.
The manner of wrapping
depended on the content of the
gift. This is an arrangement
of the *orikata* that was used to
wrap pepper, which was once
very valuable.

see page 67

蟹牡丹

Kani-botan : Crab Peonies

牡丹の花の咲く様子が、蟹がハサミを
もたげる姿に似ていることからついた
名。牡丹は中国では富貴の象徴とされ
「百花の王」として人気がありました。

The name of this pattern comes
from its blooming peonies, which
look like crabs raising their claws.
In China, the peony was a symbol
of wealth and honor. It was called
the "king of flowers" and was quite
popular.

花たとう
Flower Tato

紙の重なりが美しい八角形のたと
うです。内側が花のように開くの
で、中に小さなプレゼントを入れ
ると贈り物としても喜ばれます。

The paper overlaps beautifully
in this octagonal *tato*. It opens
like a flower from the center.
You can put a small present
inside it.

see page 68

菫
すみれ

Sumire : Violet

春に可憐な花をつけるスミレを文様化
したもの。スミレは古くから日本に自
生し、道端や野山などいたる所で見ら
れました。青紫の花色は「菫色」とい
う和名として残っています。

This is a pattern of violets, which
produce pretty flowers in the
spring. The violet has long grown
wild in Japan, and could once be
seen everywhere, from roadsides
to hills and fields. The blue-purple
color of its flowers is still called
sumire-iro (violet color) in Japan.

花模様
Flower Design

満開の花のような伝承折り紙です。飾りとして贈り物につけてもきれいです。こうした八角形のたとうは多くの種類が伝えられています。

This traditional model looks like a flower in full bloom. You can put it on a present as a pretty decoration. There are many traditional octagonal *tatos* such as this one.

see page 70

唐草

Karakusa : Arabesque

草のつるが連続する様子を図案化した
もの。唐草とは「中国の草」を意味し
ますが、ルーツは古代オリエントやギ
リシャの文様に見られ、シルクロード
を経て中国から伝わった文様です。

This is a patttern of interwoven
grass vines. *Karakusa* means
Chinese grass, but the roots of this
pattern are in the ancient orient
and Greece. It entered China
via the Silk Road and was then
introduced to Japan.

六角たとう
Hexagonal Tato

六角形を基本にした少し不思議な
形のたとうです。上の三角を引く
と中が開き、小物を入れることも
できます。

This *tato* has a bit of a curious
shape based on a hexagon. By
pulling on the triangles on
top, you can open it and put
something small inside.

see page 72

秋草

Akikusa : Fall Grasses

秋の草花のうち、ハギ、キク、ススキ
を図案化したもの。「秋草文様」は着
物の柄や昔の焼きものの絵付けに多く
見られ、秋の野に草花が寄り添うよう
な風情が好まれました。

This is a pattern of three fall
grasses and flowers: *hagi* (bush
clover), *kiku* (chrysanthemum),
and *susuki* (silver grass). The
akikusa pattern was often used for
kimonos and pictured on ceramic
ware. Scenes of fall grasses and
flowers nestled on fall fields were
popular.

熨斗付きぽち袋
Pochi Bag with Noshi

小銭を少しだけ（これっぽっち）入れてあるという意味で「ぽち袋」といいます。熨斗は昔、贈り物に添えた「のしあわび」のこと。

This is called a *pochi* bag because it holds just a little change (*koreppochi* means "just a little" in Japanese). The *noshi* is a traditional paper decoration for gifts.

see page 74

亀甲花菱

Kikko-hanabishi
: Turtle Shell Flower Chestnut

連続する六角形は亀の甲羅に似ている
ことから亀甲と呼ばれ、これは中に花
菱（菱形の花模様）を入れた文様。平
安貴族がその官位に応じて装束に用
いた「有職文様」の一つです。

Patterns of hexagons are called *kikko*
(turtle shell), because they look like
the shell of a turtle. In this pattern,
there are *hanabishi* (diamond-shaped
flower designs) in the hexagons. This
is a court pattern that Heian era
nobility used on attire to indicate
status.

たとうのぽち袋

Tato Pouch

四角に折るもっとも基本的なたとうです。大きさを変えた紙で折れば、洋服、絵、CD、お金などを贈るときに応用できます。

This is the most basic square *tato*. By folding it using different sized papers, you can wrap gifts of clothing, pictures, CDs, money and more.

see page 75

裾蝶

Suso-cho : Hem Butterfly

「裾鶴」(18ページ)同様、下(裾)から
上へ蝶の群れが舞う華麗な文様です。
蝶の文様は平安時代には貴族に、鎌倉
時代以降は武士階級に好まれ、家紋に
も用いられています。

As with *suso-tsuru* (page 18), this
is a glamorous pattern in which a
group of butterflies are dancing up
from the bottom (hem). Butterfly
patterns were preferred by nobility
in the Heian era and by the
samurai class from the Kamakura
era on, and were also used for
family crests.

糸入れ
Thread Case

これは「糸入れ」として昔から伝
わる四角いたとう。中に糸を入れ、
糸口を出して使います。男の子は
「めんこ」にも使いました。

This square *tato* was
traditionally used as a thread
case. To use, put thread inside
and pull one end out from the
top. Boys also used this model
to play a card game called
menko.

see page 76

子持格子

Komochi-goshi : Grid with Child

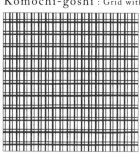

縦横に線を交差させた柄を格子とい
い、江戸時代には歌舞伎役者が好んだ
影響で大変流行しました。これは太線
の隣に細線があるのを親子に見立てて
「子持格子」といいます。

Patterns of crossing lines are
called *koshi* (grid), and became
very popular in the Edo era due to
kabuki actors favoring them. This
pattern is called *komochi-goshi*
(grid with child) because there
is a thin line next to the fat line,
resembling a parent and child.

菊皿

Kikuzara

星のような形の伝承折り紙です。
菓子皿にも使えますが、七夕祭り
やパーティーの飾りつけとしても
おなじみです。

This is a traditional model that
looks like a star. It can be used
to hold sweets, but is most
commonly used as a decoration
for Tanabata (Star Festival)
celebrations and parties.

see page 77

菊つなぎ

Kiku-tsunagi : Linked Chrysanthemum

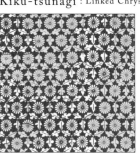

菊花を葉で囲み連続させた文様です。菊は中国の菊水や菊花酒（不老長寿の妙薬という）の影響で長寿の象徴とされます。また菊花紋は天皇・皇族の紋章。日本の旅券にも使われています。

This is an unbroken pattern of *kiku* (chrysanthemum) flowers surrounded by leaves. *Kiku* symbolize long life in China, due to the influence of *kiku* water and *kiku* alcohol (considered anti-aging, long life remedies). A *kiku* flower crest is used by Japan's imperial family, and appears on Japanese passports.

着物と
鶴のぽち袋
Kimono and
Crane Pouches

1枚の紙から鶴と着物の形のぽち
袋が作れます。着物の折り紙は、
還暦のお祝いで赤飯に添える「胡
麻塩包み」を原形にしています。

You can make both a crane
pouch and kimono pouch from
a single piece of paper. The
kimono pouch was originally
used to wrap the salt and
sesame that was served with
festive red rice at 60th birthday
celebrations.

see page 78-79

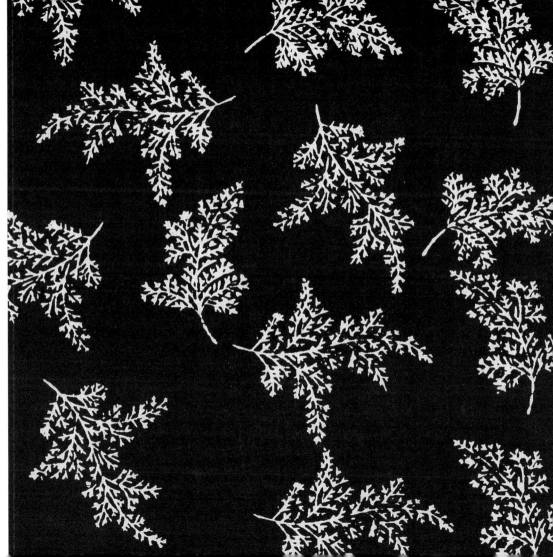

<ruby>忍草<rt>しのぶぐさ</rt></ruby>

Shinobu-gusa : Endurance Grass

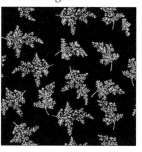

シダ類の一種の「忍草」(シノブ、ノキ
シノブなど別名あり)をそのまま拓本
にしたような文様です。「忍草」は水
がなくなっても踏まれても耐え忍び、
枯れないことから付いた名。

In this pattern, it is as if an ink
impression of *shinobu-gusa* (a type
of fern) has been made on the
paper. *Shinobu-gusa* (endurance
grass) is so called because these
ferns can endure both not having
water and being stepped on
without wilting.

豆皿入れ
Mamezara Holder

陶磁器のごく小さな皿を豆皿とい
い、時代の古いものは収集家に人
気があります。これはその豆皿を
贈るときに使われる折り方です。

Mamezara are mini ceramic
plates, and antiques are popular
with collectors. This model is
used when giving someone a
mamezara.

see page 80

纏
まとい

Matoi : Firemen's Banners

江戸の町火消しが使った「纏」の意匠
を集めた文様。二番三番などは担当地
域を表わし、「消し」にかけた芥子の
実の飾りも見られます。「火事は江戸
の華」で、一番乗りして纏をふるう纏
持ちはヒーローでした。

This pattern is a collection of the
designs used on banners carried by loc
firemen in Edo (old Tokyo). The No. 2
(二番), No. 3 (三番) and so on indicate
the area a group was in charge of.
Banners were sometimes decorated wi
keshi (poppy seeds). *Keshi* means both
poppy seed and put out in Japanese.
There were many fires in Edo, and the
banner holder, who arrived first wavin
the banner, was a hero.

薬包み

Medicine Pouch

粉薬や丸薬を入れて薬局などで実
際に使われていた折り方です。中
国にも同様の包み方があるようで
す。スパイスなどに利用できます。

This pouch was used by
chemists to hold powdered
medicine and pills. It seems
there are similar wrapping
methods in China. It can be
used to hold spices and more.

see page 81

三色縞

Sanshoku-jima : Three-colored Str

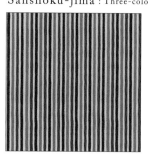

南蛮貿易で入ってきた縦縞の綿布は
南方諸島特産のため「島もの」と呼ば
れ、のちに「縞」の字があてられました。
江戸後期には縦縞の着物が大流行し、
浮世絵にも多く見られます。

Cotton fabrics with vertical stripes
were imported from Southeast Asia.
Since they came from the southern
islands, they were called *shima-mono*
(island things). Stripes soon came to
be called *shima*, which means both
stripe and island. In the latter half
of the Edo era, vertically striped
kimonos were extremely popular,
and can often be seen in ukiyo-e
pictures.

八角たとう
Octagonal Tato

「花たとう」の一種。作ってみると
紙を折り重ねて出来上がるたとう
の面白さがわかります。小物を入
れて贈ることもできます。

This is one of the flower *tatos*.
When making this, you'll see
what fun it is to create a *tato* by
folding and overlapping paper.
You can put small gifts in it.

see page 82

六角つなぎ

Rokkaku-tsunagi : Linked Hexago

雪花（雪の結晶）風の六角形を細かく
つないだ一風変わった文様です。蜂の
巣状の六角つなぎは亀甲文様にも見ら
れますが、これは比較的時代の新しい
ものです。

This is an unusual design of closely
linked hexagons that look like
snowflakes. A similar honeycomb
pattern, which is relatively modern,
can also be seen in *kikko* (turtle shell
patterns.

折据
おりすえ

Orisue

「折据」は香道の組香という遊戯で、香りを当てる際の投票箱のようなもの。茶席の遊戯（茶歌舞伎など）にも使われます。本来は厚紙で作り、昔は旅行用の裁縫箱にも利用されました。

The *orisue* is similar to a box used to hold the name of fragrances in a fragrance guessing games called *kumiko*. It is also used for tea room games (such as *chakabuki*). It was originally made from thick paper and sometimes used to hold traveling sewing kits in the old days.

see page 84

博多縞

Hakata-jima : Hakata Stripes

帯によく使われる「博多織」は、独鈷と
華皿という仏具を図案化し、縞を組み
合わせた文様が特徴。江戸時代には幕
府への献上品とされました。「博多縞」
はその文様（献上柄）を模したものです。

The *hakata* weave, which is often
used for obi, represents Buddhist
devotional tools (flower plates
and wand amulets). It is typically
combined with stripes. In the Edo
era, cloth of this weave could be
presented to the shogunate. These
hakata stripes imitate that pattern.

紅入れ
べに

Beni pouch

昔、口紅には紅（ベニバナなどを
原料とした顔料）を水で練って使い
ました。これはその紅入れの折り
紙。ティッシュや小物を入れて使
えます。

In the past, *beni* (red pigment
made from safflowers and so on)
was mixed well with water and
used as lip rouge. This model
was used to hold *beni*. It can be
also be used to hold tissues and
other small things.

see pages 85

槍梅

Yari-ume : Spear Plums

梅は奈良時代以前に中国から伝わり、
日本で広く愛された花の一つ。枝を槍
のようにまっすぐ立てた図柄を「槍梅」
といい、これは枝をとくに密集させた
もの。丸い部分が梅の花です。

Ume (Japanese plum) trees were
introduced from China before the
Nara era. Ume flowers were much
loved across Japan. Patterns of
straight *ume* branches like spears
(*yari*) are called *yari-ume*, and in the
pattern here the branches are quite
dense. The round points seem to be
ume flowers.

バラ

Rose

菓子包みなどに使うたとうをもと
にしたバラの花。バラは西洋種の
花として明治以降人気が高まり、
今では日本は世界的なバラ大国
です。

This rose is based on a *tato* that
was used to wrap sweets and so
on. The rose became popular as
a western flower after the Meiji
Restoration, and now Japan is a
major rose producing nation.

see page 86

匹田鹿の子
Hitta-kanoko

子鹿の背の斑点のような連続文様を「鹿の子」といい、鹿の子を隙間なく詰めたものを「匹田鹿の子」といいます。着物地では細かな手作業で絞り染めにし、「匹田絞り」「総鹿の子」とも呼ばれます。

A continuous pattern of spots like those on a fawn's back is called *kanoko*. If there is no space between the spots, it is called *hitta-kanoko*. Kimono fabrics are delicately tie-died by hand to make this pattern, which may also be called *hitta-shibori* or *so-kanoko*.

鶴のたとう
Crane Tato

三角折りのたとうをひと工夫して
鶴になりました。鶴は慶事につき
ものなので、お年玉やご祝儀をあ
げるときにも使えます。

With just a little work, this
triangular *tato* becomes a crane.
The paper crane is used on happy
occasions, such as when giving
gifts of money on New Year's
Day.

see page 87

唐松

Karamatsu : Chinese Pines

常緑の松は長寿や無病息災に通じる縁起のよい木とされています。唐松（中国風の松）は松葉が放射状に丸く描かれ、ここでは花火のように大胆に散らしています。

The pine tree, an evergreen, is a lucky tree that is said to bring long life and sound health. *Karamatsu* (Chinese pines) is a pattern of pine needles drawn radially in circles, which are scattered about boldly like fireworks here.

鶴の入れもの
Crane Mini Box

鶴の胴が小箱になる伝承折り紙。
鶴は長寿やめでたいことのシンボ
ルで、折り紙でもっとも多く登場
する生きものです。

This is a traditional model in
which the crane's torso becomes
a mini box. The crane, a symbol
of long life and happy events,
is the most common origami
animal.

see page 88

花丸紋重ね

Hana Marumon-kasane
: Overlapping Flower Crests

花をモチーフにした丸紋を花丸紋といいます。これは有職文様の「菊浮線」（菊の花と唐草を丸の中に配した文様）の一種をスタンプのように刷り重ねた文様です。

Circles with flower motifs are called *hana marumon*. In this pattern, one of the *kiku* (chrysanthemum) relief court patterns (*kiku* and Chinese grasses in circles) has been overprinted like stamps.

角香箱
Tsuno-kobako

伝承折り紙の一つで、菓子入れなどによく使われます。香箱とは、香道に用いる道具を入れる漆塗りの箱のこと。

This traditional model is often used to hold sweets and so on. A *kobako* is a lacquered box used to hold tools for *kodo*, the ancient Japanese art of appreciating incense.

see page 90

源氏香ちらし
Genjiko-chirashi

香道で使う「源氏香の図」と草花を文様にしたもの。源氏香は「組香(くみこう)」の一種で、五種の香を聞き分け、「源氏香の図」(縦5本の線で52通りの組合わせを書いた図)と照合して「源氏物語」の巻名で答えるという雅びな遊びです。

Here, the *genjiko* diagrams used in *kodo* have been made into a pattern with flowers. *Genjiko* was a sophisticated fragrance guessing game in which five scents were described, reference made to a *genjiko* diagram (a diagram with 52 smell combinations drawn using five vertical lines) and answers given as chapter names from *The Tale of Genji*.

うさぎ
兎の粉包み
Rabbit Flour Wrapper

昔、武家の間で餅を贈るときはき
な粉を添えました。これはそのき
な粉を入れる「折形」を元にアレ
ンジした折り紙です。兎に見立て
た遊び心が伝わってきます。

In the old days, when *mochi*
(sticky rice cakes) were given
as presents between samurai
families, *kinako* (soybean flour
topping) was included. This
model is an arrangement of
the *orikata* used to wrap that
soybean flour. It looks like a
rabbit and conveys a sense of
fun.

see page 91

小花

Kobana : Small Flowers

一面に小菊と五弁の小花を散らして
あります。小さな花を全面にあしらう
文様は江戸末期から増え、千代紙や着
物の柄など庶民にもなじみの深いもの
です。

This pattern has small
chrysanthemums and other flowers
scattered on one side. Patterns of
small flowers scattered across a
whole surface proliferated in the
latter half of the Edo era. They
were used as *chiyogami* and kimono
patterns, and were very familiar to
regular people.

花箱
Flower Box

花が咲いたように見える箱状の折
り紙で、もとは中国で伝承された
もの。ビーズなどを小分けして整
理するのにも使えます。

This boxed-shaped model looks
like a blooming flower and is of
ancient Chinese origin. It can
be used to organize beads and
so on.

see page 92

さがり藤
Sagari-fuji : Hanging Wisteria

藤の花は平安時代後期の藤原氏の繁
栄とともに格が上がり、有職文様に用
いられるようになりました。房状の花
の柄が映えるため、女性の着物や帯地
の文様にも好まれました。

The rank of *fuji* (wisteria) flowers rose
in the latter half of the Heian era
along with the fortunes of the
Fujiwara clan, and they soon came
to be used in court patterns. As the
tufts of flowers stand out, they were
popular on women's kimonos and
obis.

六角の菓子鉢
Hexagonal Sweets Box

底を作って折り上げる六角形の立
体たとう。一見現代風ですが、昔
から伝わる折り方です。誕生祝い
を入れて贈っても喜ばれます。

This three dimensional
hexagonal *tato* is made by
creating the bottom and then
folding up. At first glance it
looks modern, but it is actually a
very old model. It makes a great
box for birthday presents.

see page 93

亀甲

Kikko : Turtle Shell

古くから西アジアなどでも見られる正
六角形の幾何文様。日本では、長寿の
象徴とされる亀の甲羅に似ていること
から「亀甲」と呼ばれて吉祥文となり、
有職文様として用いられました。

This is a geometric pattern of regular
hexagons that has long been used in
Western Asia. Because it resembles
the shell of a turtle, which is a symbol
of long life in Japan, it was called
kikko (turtle shell) and became a lucky
pattern. It was used as a court pattern

斜め帯のぽち袋
Diagonally Belted Pouch

お年玉や心付けを渡すときすぐ折れるぽち袋です。ぽち袋には、小銭でも裸のまま渡すのをさける日本人の気づかいが表れています。

This pouch can be folded in a snap when giving New Year's money or tips. It expresses the consideration of Japanese people, who avoid giving even small change without first wrapping it.

see page 94

りんどう

Rindo : Dragon Bile

秋に紫色の花を咲かせる草花。漢方薬にも使い、苦みが強く「竜の胆のよう」ということから「竜胆」の名が付きました。家紋にも使われ、葉が笹に似ているので「笹りんどう」の名でも呼ばれます。

Rindo is a purple flower that blooms in fall. It is used in Chinese herbal medicine, and is called *rindo* (dragon bile) because it as bitter as the bile of a dragon! It is also used as a family crest, and sometimes called *sasa* (bamboo grass) *rindo*, because it's leaves looks like bamboo grass.

水鳥の入れもの
Waterbird Box

優雅に泳ぐ水鳥の姿は折り紙の
素材として昔から人気があります。
キャンディーなどを入れてテーブ
ルに置いても素敵です。

Waterbirds, which swim
elegantly, have long been
popular origami subjects. This
box makes a lovely candy holder
you can put on your table.

see page 95

荒波

Aranami : Rough Waves

自然現象を図案化したものを天象地文
様といい、これは海の荒波を意匠化し
たもの。寄せては返す雄々しさが戦国
武将や武士階級に好まれ、武具や旗印
などにも使われました。

Stylized patterns of natural
phenomena are called celestial
patterns. This pattern represents
the rough waves of the ocean. It
was popular with military
commanders and the samurai class
in the age of provincial wars, who
liked the bravery of the waves'
approach and retreat, and was
used on armor and flags.

基本の折り方
Basic Folds

よく使う折り方です。とくに「四角折り」や「中わり折り」はよく使います。
These are the most common folds, especially the square base and the inside reverse fold.

四角折り Square base

1 谷折り線、山折り線の折りすじをつける
Make valley and mountain creases as shown.

2 ★と★、☆と☆がつくようにたたむ
Fold to bring the matching star points together.

3 できあがり
Finished!

中わり折り Inside reverse fold

1 折りすじをつける
Make a crease as shown.

2 紙のさきを、内側に入れるように折る
Push the point between the layers and fold in.

3 できあがり
Finished!

ざぶとん折り Blintz base

1 中心をつくる
Make a center point.

2 4つのかどを中心に向かって折る
Fold all four corners to the center.

3 できあがり
Finished!

かぶせ折り Outside reverse fold

1 折りすじをつける
Make a crease as shown.

2 紙を上にかぶせるように折る
Fold the paper over as shown.

3 できあがり
Finished!

※中心のしるしのつけ方　軽く半分に折って、真ん中をおさえてもどす。別の向きから軽く半分に折って、真ん中をおさえてもどす。×印がついたところが紙の中心
How to make the center point:　Fold the paper in half lightly and pinch the center, then open. Repeat from the opposite direction. The resulting cross mark is the center point.

四角たとう Square Tato [see page 17]

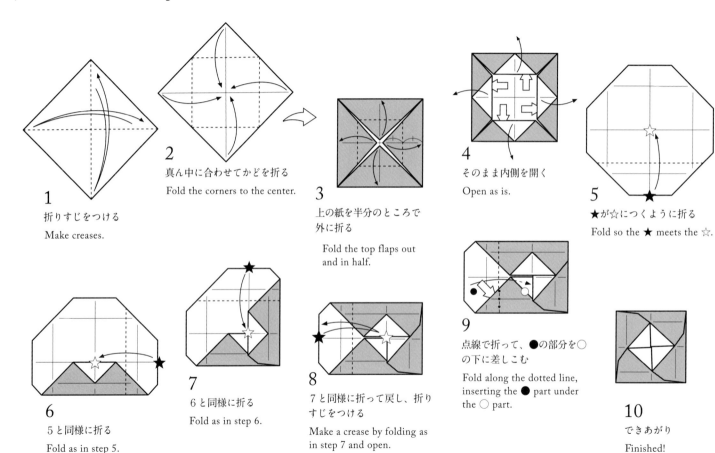

1
折りすじをつける
Make creases.

2
真ん中に合わせてかどを折る
Fold the corners to the center.

3
上の紙を半分のところで
外に折る
Fold the top flaps out
and in half.

4
そのまま内側を開く
Open as is.

5
★が☆につくように折る
Fold so the ★ meets the ☆.

6
5と同様に折る
Fold as in step 5.

7
6と同様に折る
Fold as in step 6.

8
7と同様に折って戻し、折り
すじをつける
Make a crease by folding as
in step 7 and open.

9
点線で折って、●の部分を○
の下に差しこむ
Fold along the dotted line,
inserting the ● part under
the ○ part.

10
できあがり
Finished!

胡椒包み Pepper Wrapper [see page 19]

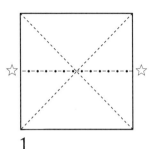

1
図のように折りすじをつける

Make creases as shown.

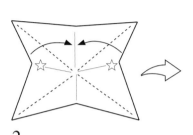

2
☆と☆がつくようにたたむ
（三角折り）

Fold so the ☆s meet (triangle base).

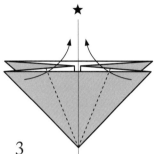

3
上の1枚を★の中心線に
合わせて折る

Fold the top flaps so they meet the centerline.

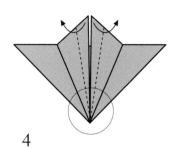

4
真ん中から3分の1のところ
で斜めに折る

Fold out about 1/3 from the middle.

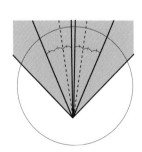

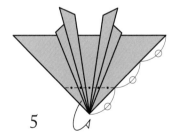

5
下から3分の1の
あたりで山折りする

Mountain fold about 1/3 from the bottom.

6
できあがり

Finished!

花たとう Flower Tato [see page 21]

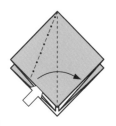

1

「四角折り」（65 ページ）から
はじめる。折りすじをつけて、
開いてつぶす（4 か所）

Begin with a square base
(page 65). Make creases,
open and squash (all four
flaps).

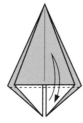

2

折りすじをつけてから
全体を開く

Make creases and then open.

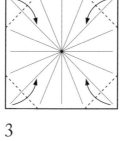

3

点線でかどを折る

Fold the corners along the
dotted lines.

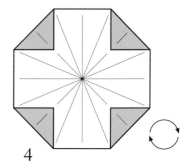

4

折ったところ

Make this shape.

5

☆が★（中心）につくように
折って、図のように折りすじ
をつける（8 か所）。下の 1 か
所を真ん中まで折る
（図 6 参照）

Fold so the ☆ meets the ★
(center) to make creases as
shown (all eight corners).
Fold the bottom corner to
the center (see step 6).

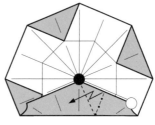

6

○が●につくように折る
（図 7 参照）

Fold so the ○ meets the ●
(see step 7).

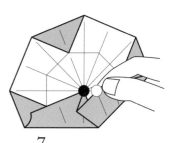

7

途中の図

In progress.

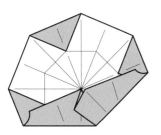

8

折ったところ
残りのかど（6か所）も同じにする

Make this shape.
Fold the remaining six corners
in the same way.

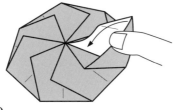

9

最後はそのままかどを押さえ
る（紙を下に差しこまない）

Push the last corner down as
is (do not insert below).

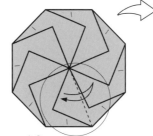

10

折りすじをつける

Make creases.

11

さらに折りすじをつける
Make creases.

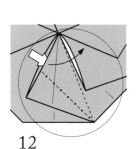

12

あいだを開いてつぶす
Open and squash.

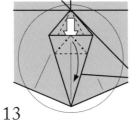

13

あいだを開いて手前にたおす
Open and fold down.

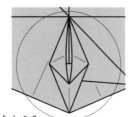

14

折ったところ
残りの7か所も
10～14まで同様にする

Make this shape.
Repeat steps 10 to 14 on
the other seven flaps.

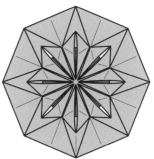

15

できあがり
Finished!

花模様 Flower Design [see page 23]

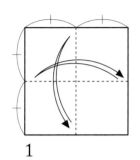

1
折りすじをつける
Make creases.

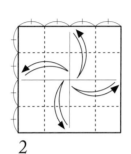

2
さらに折りすじをつける
Make creases.

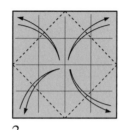

3
三角の折りすじをつける
Make triangular creases.

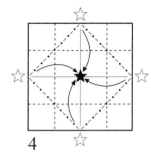

4
☆が★（中央）につくように
折り線どおりにたたむ
Fold along the creases so the
☆s meet the ★(center).

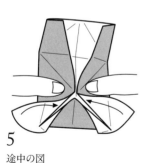

5
途中の図
In progress.

6
途中の図。上に四角が4つできる
In progress. Four squares are made.

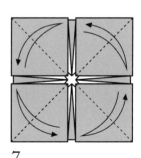

7
上の1枚のみ折りすじをつける（4か所）
Make creases on the top flaps only
(all four flaps).

※指が入りにくいときは
楊枝などを利用する

If your fingers don't fit
well, use a toothpick.

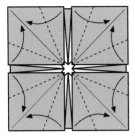

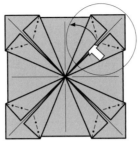

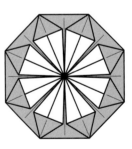

8

7でつけた折りすじに合わせ
て、はしを折る

Fold the edges in along the
creases made in step 7.

9

8で折ったところを、あいだを
開いて三角につぶす（8か所）

Open the flaps from step 8,
and squash into triangles (all
eight flaps).

10

拡大図

Enlargement.

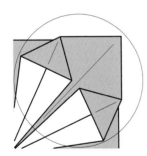

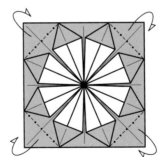

11

開いたところ

After opening.

12

4つのかどを三角に折る

Fold the four corners back.

13

できあがり

Finished!

六角たとう Hexagonal Tato [see page 25]

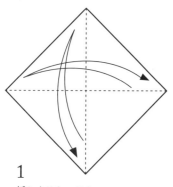

1
折りすじをつける
Make creases.

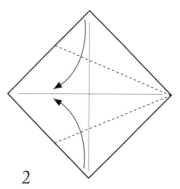

2
線に合わせてかどを折る
Fold the corners to the line.

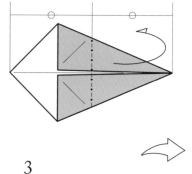

3
半分のところで山折りする
Mountain fold in half.

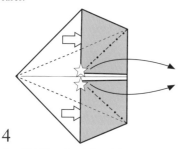

4
あいだを開いて、☆をつまむ
ようにして折り線どおりに折る
Pinching the ☆s, open and
fold along the creases.

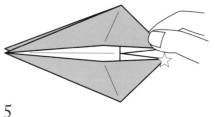

5
途中の図
In progress.

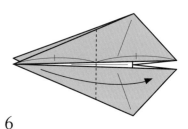

6
上の1枚のみ半分に折る
Fold the top flap only in half.

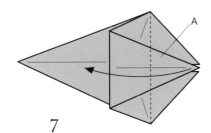

7

全体に折りすじをつけてからA
のみ谷折りする
（うらも6、7を同様に）

After making a full crease, valley
fold A only (repeat steps 6 and 7
on the back).

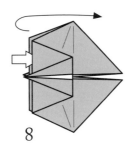

8

あいだを開いて、うしろの
部分を右にたおす

Open and fold the back part
to the right.

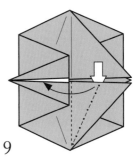

9

折りすじをつけて、あいだを
開いてつぶす

Make creases, open and
squash.

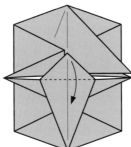

10

三角の部分を点線で谷折りする

Valley fold the triangular part
along the dotted line.

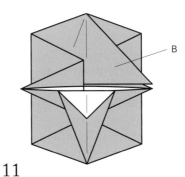

11

Bも9、10を同様にする

Repeat steps 9 and 10 on B.

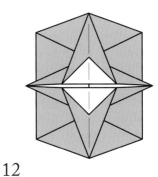

12

できあがり

Finished!

熨斗付きぽち袋　Pochi Bag with Noshi [see page 27]

[see page 27]

図中の数字は 15cm 角の紙で折るときの目安です。
Figures in the diagram are for the case of a 15 x 15 cm piece of paper

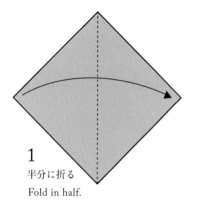

1
半分に折る
Fold in half.

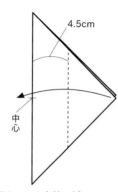

4.5cm

中心

2
中心に印をつけて点線で折る
Mark the center and fold
along the dotted line.

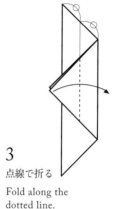

3
点線で折る
Fold along the
dotted line.

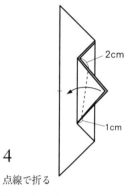

2cm

1cm

4
点線で折る
Fold along the
dotted line.

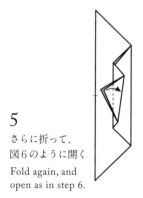

5
さらに折って、
図6のように開く
Fold again, and
open as in step 6.

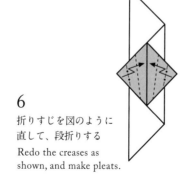

6
折りすじを図のように
直して、段折りする
Redo the creases as
shown, and make pleats.

A

B

7
A、Bの順に山折りして、
AをBの中に差しこむ
Mountain fold A and
then B. Insert A into B.

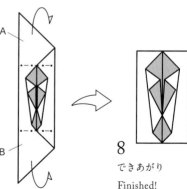

8
できあがり
Finished!

たとうのぽち袋 Tato Pouch [see page 29]

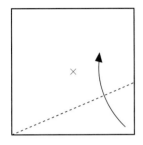

1

中心に印をつけて、斜めに中
心まで折る

Mark the center, then fold
diagonally to the center.

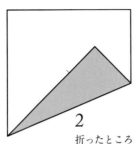

2

折ったところ
戻してほかの3か所も同様に
折りすじをつける

Make this shape.
Open and make creases on
the other three sides.

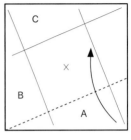

3

ABC の順に折り線どおりに
たたむ

Fold along crease A, B and
then C.

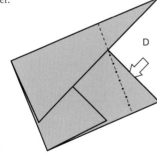

4

最後はDを2でつけた折り線どおり
にたたみながら、下の部分を折りこむ

Finally, fold D along the crease made
in step 2, folding the lower part in.

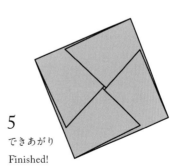

5

できあがり
Finished!

糸入れ Thread Case [see page 31]

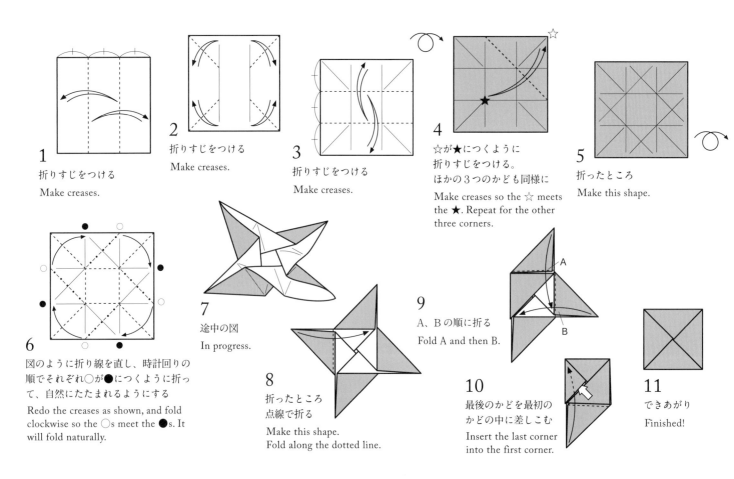

1
折りすじをつける
Make creases.

2
折りすじをつける
Make creases.

3
折りすじをつける
Make creases.

4
☆が★につくように
折りすじをつける。
ほかの3つのかども同様に
Make creases so the ☆ meets
the ★. Repeat for the other
three corners.

5
折ったところ
Make this shape.

6
図のように折り線を直し、時計回りの
順でそれぞれ○が●につくように折っ
て、自然にたたまれるようにする
Redo the creases as shown, and fold
clockwise so the ○s meet the ●s. It
will fold naturally.

7
途中の図
In progress.

8
折ったところ
点線で折る
Make this shape.
Fold along the dotted line.

9
A、Bの順に折る
Fold A and then B.

10
最後のかどを最初の
かどの中に差しこむ
Insert the last corner
into the first corner.

11
できあがり
Finished!

菊皿 Kikuzara [see page 33]

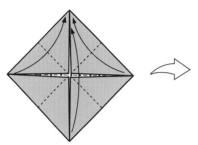

1

「ざぶとん折り」(65 ページ) からはじめる。折り
すじをつけて「四角折り」(65 ページ) をする

Begin with the blintz base (page 65). Make
creases and make a square base (page 65).

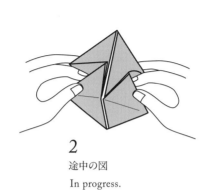

2

途中の図

In progress.

3

図のように折りすじをつけてからあいだを開いて
たたむ (図4参照)。うらも同じに

After making creases as shown, open and fold
down (see step 4).

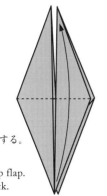

4

上の1枚を谷折りする。
うらも同じに

Valley fold the top flap.
Repeat on the back.

5

先端を左右に開く

Open the tips to the right
and left.

6

開いているところ

Opening.

7

できあがり

Finished!

着物のぽち袋 Kimono Pouch [see page 35] ✂

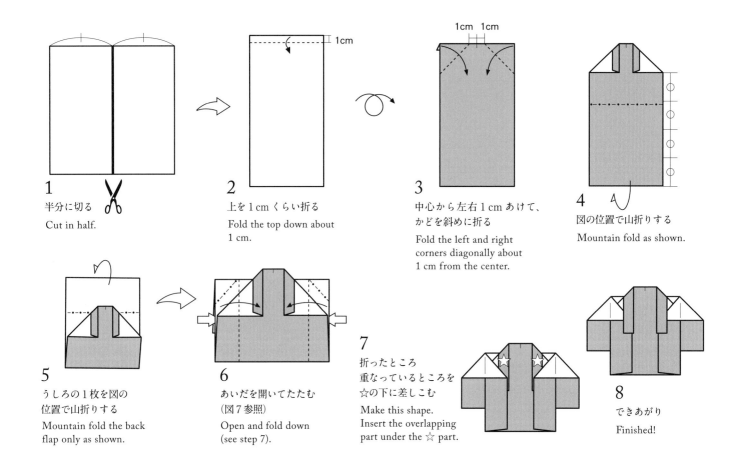

1
半分に切る
Cut in half.

2
上を1cmくらい折る
Fold the top down about 1 cm.

1cm

3
中心から左右1cmあけて、かどを斜めに折る
Fold the left and right corners diagonally about 1 cm from the center.

1cm 1cm

4
図の位置で山折りする
Mountain fold as shown.

5
うしろの1枚を図の位置で山折りする
Mountain fold the back flap only as shown.

6
あいだを開いてたたむ（図7参照）
Open and fold down (see step 7).

7
折ったところ重なっているところを☆の下に差しこむ
Make this shape. Insert the overlapping part under the ☆ part.

8
できあがり
Finished!

鶴のぽち袋 Crane Pouch [see page 35]

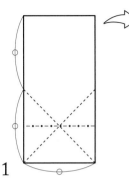

1

半分の紙を図のように折り
すじをつけて、「三角折り」
（67ページ）をする

On half the paper, make
creases as shown and make a
triangle base (page 67).

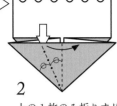

2

上の1枚のみ折りすじ
をつけて、あいだを開
いてたたむ

Crease the top flap only,
open and fold down.

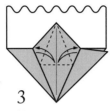

3

折りすじをつける

Make creases.

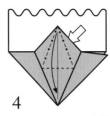

4

あいだを開いて、手前
にたおしてたたむ
（図5参照）

Open and fold down
(see step 5).

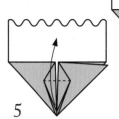

5

谷折りして折り上げる

Valley fold up.

6

左にたおす

Fold to the left.

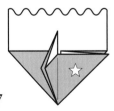

7

☆の部分も2〜5まで同じに
する。6で右にたおす

Fold the ☆ part as in steps 2
to 5, but in step 6 fold to the
right.

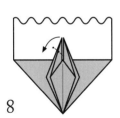

8

「中わり折り」（65ページ）
をして頭をつくる

Make the head with an inside
reverse fold (page 65).

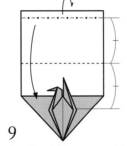

9

上を少し山折りしてから図の
位置で折り鶴のうしろに差し
こむ

Mountain fold on the top a
little and insert behind the
paper crane as shown.

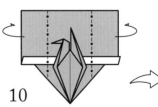

10

両側をうしろで重なるように
山折りし、片方をもう一方に
差しこむ

Mountain fold so the sides
overlap in the back, and
insert one side into the other.

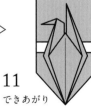

11

できあがり

Finished!

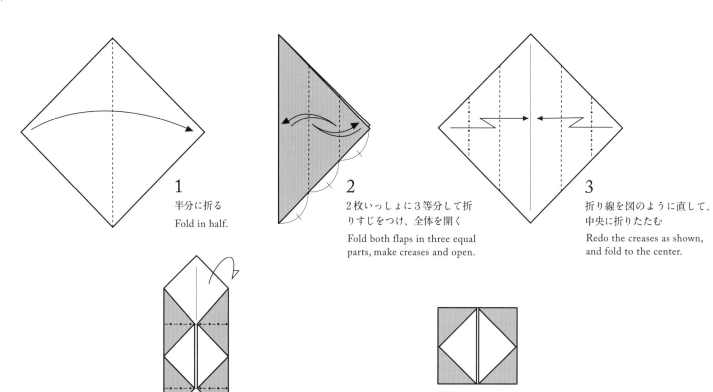

豆皿入れ Mamezara Holder [see page 37]

1
半分に折る
Fold in half.

2
2枚いっしょに3等分して折りすじをつけ、全体を開く
Fold both flaps in three equal parts, make creases and open.

3
折り線を図のように直して、中央に折りたたむ
Redo the creases as shown, and fold to the center.

4
上、下の順に山折りする
Mountain fold the top and then the bottom.

5
できあがり
Finished!

薬包み Medicine Pouch [see page 39]

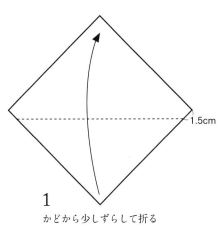

1

かどから少しずらして折る

Fold a little below the center line.

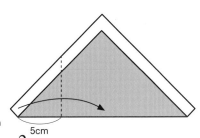

—1.5cm

5cm

2

はしから5cmくらいのところ
で折る

Fold about 5 cm from the
end.

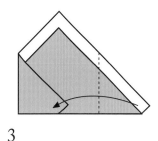

3

右側も同様に折って、真ん中
で少し重ねる

Fold the right side in the
same way, overlapping a little
in the middle.

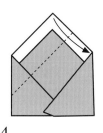

4

点線で折る

Fold along the dotted line.

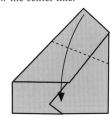

5

重ねるように斜めに折る

Fold diagonally and overlap.

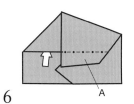

A

6

Aの部分を下に折りこむ

Fold A under.

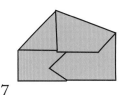

7

できあがり

Finished!

八角たとう Octagonal Tato [see page 41]

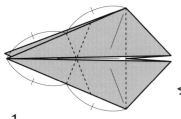

1

「六角たとう」（72ページ）の6からはじめる。図のように3か所に折りすじをつける

Begin from step 6 of the Hexagonal Tato (page 72). Make three creases as shown.

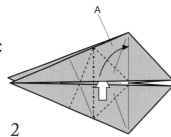

2

図のように折りすじをつけてAのみ、あいだを開いてたたむ

Make creases as shown, open A only and fold.

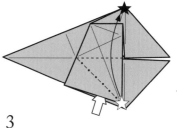

3

☆が★につくようにあいだを開いてたたむ

Open and fold so the ☆ meets the ★.

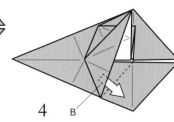

4 B

Bの中の折りたたまれた部分を引き出す

Pull out the part folded into B.

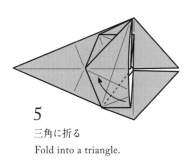

5

三角に折る

Fold into a triangle.

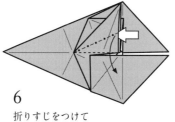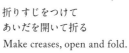

6

折りすじをつけてあいだを開いて折る

Make creases, open and fold.

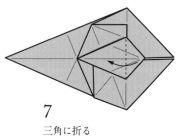

7

三角に折る

Fold into a triangle.

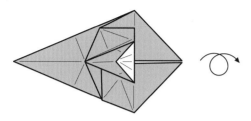

8

折ったところ。うらがえす

Make this shape. Turnover.

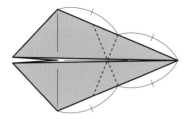

9

この側も1〜8まで同様にする

Repeat steps 1 to 8 on this side.

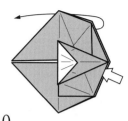

10

あいだを開いて、
うしろ側を左にたおす

Open and fold the back side to the left.

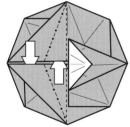

11

上下の三角を6、7と同様に
開いて折る

Fold the top and bottom triangles as in steps 6 to 7.

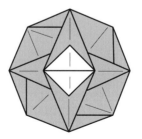

12

中心の三角を反時計回りの順
に重ねていく。

Overlap the center triangles moving anticlockwise.

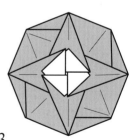

13

できあがり

Finished!

折据 Orisue [see page 43]

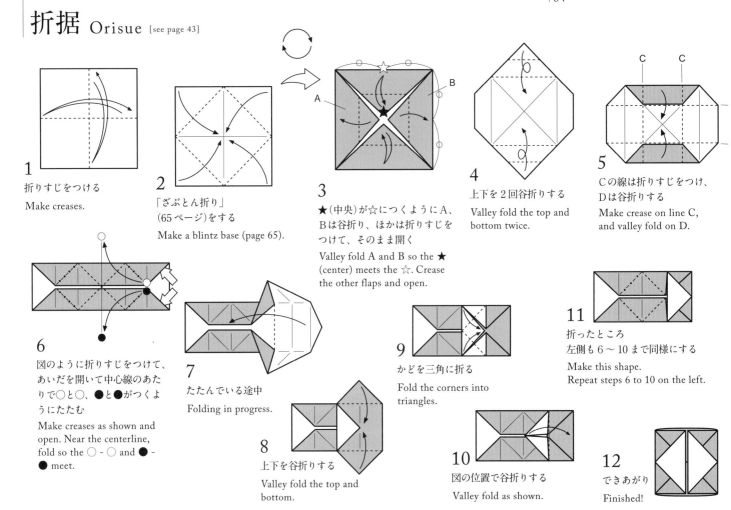

1
折りすじをつける
Make creases.

2
「ざぶとん折り」
(65 ページ)をする
Make a blintz base (page 65).

3
★(中央)が☆につくようにA、
Bは谷折り、ほかは折りすじを
つけて、そのまま開く
Valley fold A and B so the ★
(center) meets the ☆. Crease
the other flaps and open.

4
上下を2回谷折りする
Valley fold the top and
bottom twice.

5
Cの線は折りすじをつけ、
Dは谷折りする
Make crease on line C,
and valley fold on D.

6
図のように折りすじをつけて、
あいだを開いて中心線のあた
りで○と○、●と●がつくよ
うにたたむ
Make creases as shown and
open. Near the centerline,
fold so the ○ - ○ and ● -
● meet.

7
たたんでいる途中
Folding in progress.

8
上下を谷折りする
Valley fold the top and
bottom.

9
かどを三角に折る
Fold the corners into
triangles.

10
図の位置で谷折りする
Valley fold as shown.

11
折ったところ
左側も6〜10まで同様にする
Make this shape.
Repeat steps 6 to 10 on the left.

12
できあがり
Finished!

紅入れ Beni Pouch [see page 45]

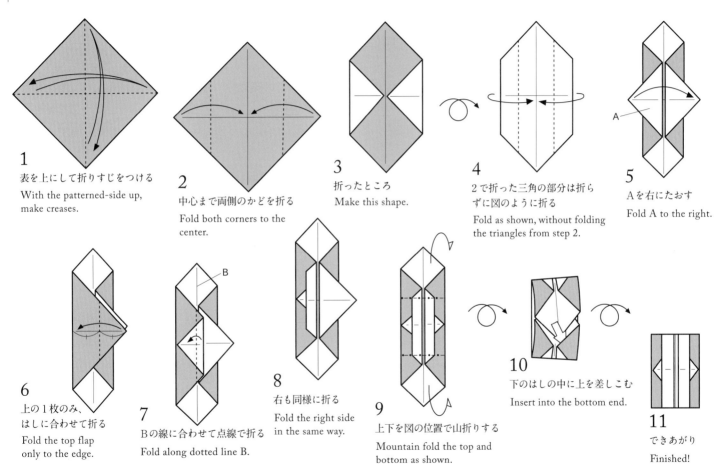

1
表を上にして折りすじをつける
With the patterned-side up, make creases.

2
中心まで両側のかどを折る
Fold both corners to the center.

3
折ったところ
Make this shape.

4
2で折った三角の部分は折らずに図のように折る
Fold as shown, without folding the triangles from step 2.

5
Aを右にたおす
Fold A to the right.

6
上の1枚のみ、はしに合わせて折る
Fold the top flap only to the edge.

7
Bの線に合わせて点線で折る
Fold along dotted line B.

8
右も同様に折る
Fold the right side in the same way.

9
上下を図の位置で山折りする
Mountain fold the top and bottom as shown.

10
下のはしの中に上を差しこむ
Insert into the bottom end.

11
できあがり
Finished!

バラ Rose [see page 47]

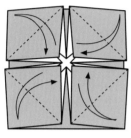

1

「花模様」（70 ページ）の 7 からはじめる。折りすじをつける

Begin from step 7 of the Flower Design (page 70). Make creases.

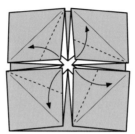

2

上の紙を 1 でつけた 折り線に合うように折る

Fold so the top flaps meet the creases made in step 1.

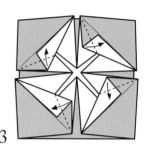

3

さらに点線で折る

Fold along the dotted lines.

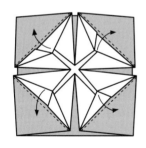

4

1 でつけた折り線で折る

Fold along the creases from step 1.

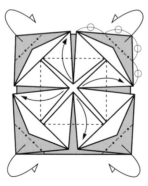

5

中心を図のように折り立てる。外側の4つのかどは半分くらいで山折りする

Fold the center as shown. Mountain fold the four outer corners in half.

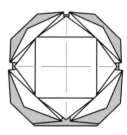

6

できあがり

Finished!

鶴のたとう Crane Tato [see page 49]

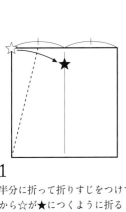

1

半分に折って折りすじをつけて
から☆が★につくように折る

Fold in half and make a
crease. Then fold so the ☆
meets the ★.

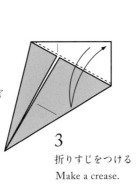

2

図のように☆が★に
つくように折る

Fold so the ☆ meets
the ★ as shown.

3

折りすじをつける

Make a crease.

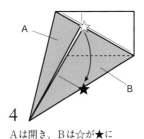

4

Aは開き、Bは☆が★に
つくように折る

Open A, and fold B so the ☆
meets the ★.

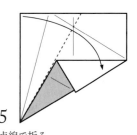

5

点線で折る

Fold along the dotted line.

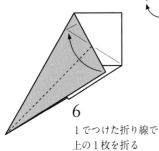

6

1でつけた折り線で
上の1枚を折る

Fold the top flap along the
crease from step 1.

7

点線で折る

Fold along
the dotted line.

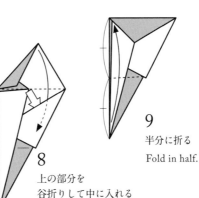

8

上の部分を
谷折りして中に入れる

Valley fold the top and insert.

9

半分に折る

Fold in half.

10

少し斜めに折って頭をつくる

Fold diagonally a little to
make the head.

11

できあがり

Finished!

※首の部分をのりでとめてもいいです。
You can glue down the neck.

鶴の入れもの Crane Mini Box [see page 51]

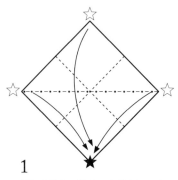

1

折りすじをつけて、☆が★につく
ように「四角折り」（65ページ）
をする

Make creases, and make a square
base (page 65) so the ☆s meet the ★.

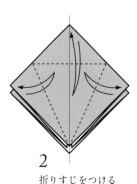

2

折りすじをつける

Make creases.

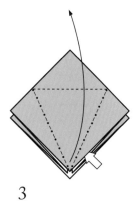

3

上の紙のあいだを開いて、
折り上げる

Open the top flap and fold up.

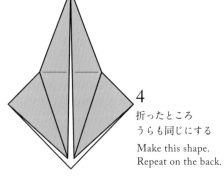

4

折ったところ
うらも同じにする

Make this shape.
Repeat on the back.

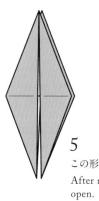

5

この形ができたら全体を開く

After making this shape,
open.

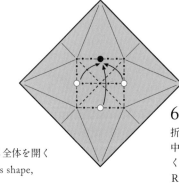

6

折り線を図のように直して、
中心をへこませ、○が●につ
くようにたたむ（図7参照）

Redo the creases as shown.
Fold so the center folds in and
the ○s meet the ● (see step 7).

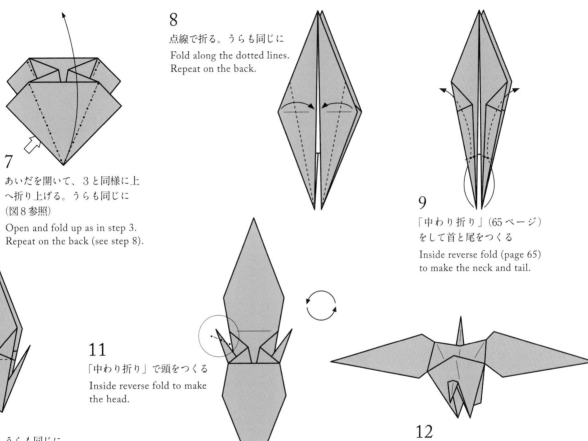

7

あいだを開いて、3と同様に上
へ折り上げる。うらも同じに
（図8参照）

Open and fold up as in step 3.
Repeat on the back (see step 8).

8

点線で折る。うらも同じに

Fold along the dotted lines.
Repeat on the back.

9

「中わり折り」（65ページ）
をして首と尾をつくる

Inside reverse fold (page 65)
to make the neck and tail.

10

羽を手前に折る。うらも同じに

Fold the wing down. Repeat
on the back.

11

「中わり折り」で頭をつくる

Inside reverse fold to make
the head.

12

できあがり

Finished!

角香箱 Tsuno-kobako [see page 53]

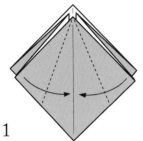

1

「四角折り」（65 ページ）か
らはじめる。
真ん中の線に合わせて折る

Begin with the square base (page
65). Fold to the centerline.

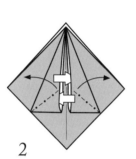

2

あいだを開いてたたむ

Open and fold.

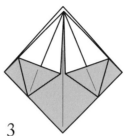

3

たたんだところ
うらも 1、2 と同様に

Make this shape. Repeat
steps 1 and 2 on the back.

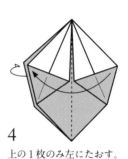

4

上の 1 枚のみ左にたおす。
うらも同じに

Fold the top flap only to the
left. Repeat on the back.

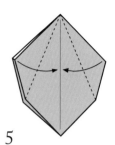

5

真ん中の線に合わせて折る
うらも同じに

Fold to the centerline.
Repeat on the back.

6

上の 1 枚のみ点線で手前に折
る。うらも同じに

Fold the top flap only down
along the dotted line.
Repeat on the back.

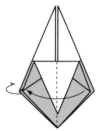

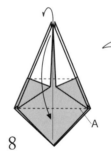

7

上の 1 枚のみ左へたおす。
うらも同じに

Fold the top flap only to the
left. Repeat on the back.

8

6 と同様に点線で折る。
A は折りすじをつける。

Fold along the dotted line as
in step 6. Make crease A.

9

あいだを開いて形を
ととのえる

Open and set the shape.

10

できあがり

Finished!

兎の粉包み Rabbit Flour Wrapper [see page 55]

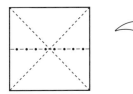

1

図のように折りすじをつけて
「三角折り」(67 ページ) をする

Make creases as shown, and
make a triangle base (page 67).

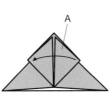

2

上の1枚を★が☆に
つくように折る

Fold the top flaps so
the ★s meet the ☆.

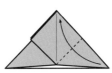

3

折りすじをつけないよう
にしてAを左へたおす

Without creasing, fold A
to the left.

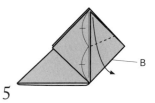

4

2と同様にかどを折る

Fold the corner as in step 2.

5

4で折った部分をBからはみ
出るように斜めに折る

Diagonally fold the part from
step 4 so it sticks out from B.

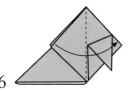

6

上の1枚のみ点線で右へたおす

Fold the top flap only to the
right along the dotted line.

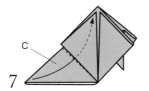

7

Cも3～6まで同様にする

Repeat steps 3 to 6 on C.

8

上の1枚のみ点線で斜めに折る

Diagonally fold the top flap
only along the dotted line.

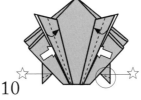

9

下をまとめて山折りする

Mountain fold the bottom.

10

耳の部分の上の1枚のみ、あいだを
開いて半分に谷折りする。下の三角
の部分も上の1枚のみ☆の線に合う
よう斜めに折り、あいだを開く

Open and valley fold the top flap
only of the ears. Diagonally fold the
top flap only of the lower triangles
along the ☆ lines, and open.

11

できあがり
Finished!

花箱 Flower Box [see page 57]

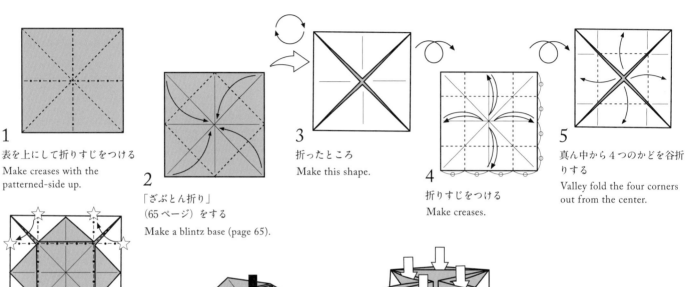

1
表を上にして折りすじをつける
Make creases with the patterned-side up.

2
「ざぶとん折り」
（65 ページ）をする
Make a blintz base (page 65).

3
折ったところ
Make this shape.

4
折りすじをつける
Make creases.

5
真ん中から4つのかどを谷折りする
Valley fold the four corners out from the center.

6
図の折り線を確認して、それぞれの☆と☆がつくように折り、立体にする
Checking the creases, fold so the ☆s meet the ☆s and it becomes 3-D.

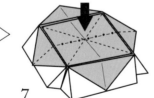

7
真ん中を押してたたむ
（図8参照）
Push the center and fold (see step 8).

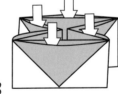

8
図のように開いて、底を広げながら上は丸く、下は四角に形をととのえる
Open as shown and spread out the bottoms, making the top round and bottom square.

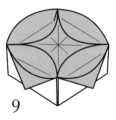

9
できあがり
Finished!

六角の菓子鉢 Hexagonal Sweets Box [see page 59]

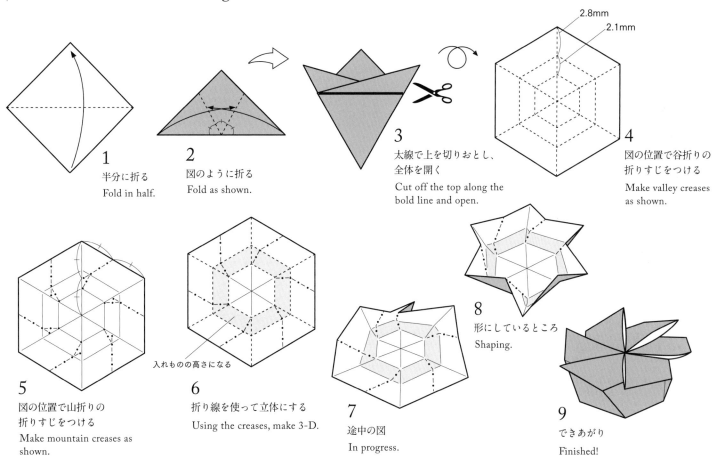

1
半分に折る
Fold in half.

2
図のように折る
Fold as shown.

3
太線で上を切りおとし、
全体を開く
Cut off the top along the
bold line and open.

4
2.8mm
2.1mm
図の位置で谷折りの
折りすじをつける
Make valley creases
as shown.

5
図の位置で山折りの
折りすじをつける
Make mountain creases as
shown.

6
入れものの高さになる
折り線を使って立体にする
Using the creases, make 3-D.

7
途中の図
In progress.

8
形にしているところ
Shaping.

9
できあがり
Finished!

斜め帯のぽち袋 Diagonally Belted Pouch [see page 61]

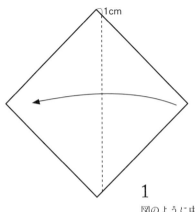

1

図のように中心から
ずらして折る
Fold away from
the center as shown.

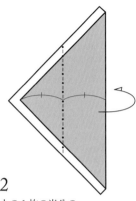

2

上の1枚の半分の
位置で山折りする
Mountain fold at
half the top flap.

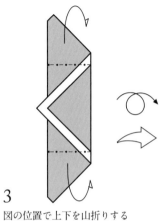

3

図の位置で上下を山折りする
Mountain fold the top and
bottom as shown.

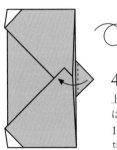

4

上の部分を下の紙の中に差しこみ
はみ出ている三角をかぶせるように折る
Insert the top into the bottom. Fold the
triangle so it is covered.

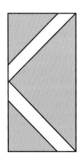

5

できあがり
Finished!

水鳥の入れもの Waterbird Box [see page 63]

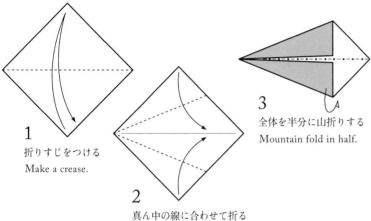

1
折りすじをつける
Make a crease.

2
真ん中の線に合わせて折る
Fold to the centerline.

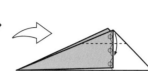

3
全体を半分に山折りする
Mountain fold in half.

4
上の1枚のみ、上から3分の1のところで谷折りする。うらも同じに
Valley fold the top flap only 1/3 from the top. Repeat on the back.

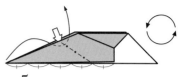

5
図の位置で折りすじをつけて「中わり折り」(65ページ)をする
Make a crease as shown, and inside reverse fold (page 65).

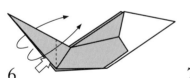

6
図の位置で折りすじをつけて「かぶせ折り」(65ページ)をする
Make a crease as shown, and outside reverse fold (page 65).

7
「かぶせ折り」で頭をつくる
Make the head with an outside reverse fold.

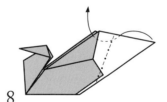

8
「中わり折り」で尾をつくる(羽の部分は折らない)
Make the tail with an inside reverse fold (don't fold the wings).

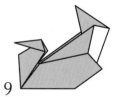

9
できあがり
Finished!

監修——小林一夫

1941年東京生まれ。内閣府認証NPO法人国際おりがみ協会理事長。お茶の水・おりがみ会館館長。全国の折り紙教室で指導や講演を行うかたわら、世界各国で折り紙や和紙を通じた国際交流、日本文化の紹介活動を行っている。著書多数。

Editorial Supervisor——**Kazuo Kobayashi**

Kazuo Kobayashi is the chairman of the International Origami Association (an incorporated nonprofit organization) and director of the Origami Center in Ochanomizu. He was born in Tokyo in 1941. He teaches and lectures origami classes all over Japan. He also organizes programs that use *washi* and origami to foster international exchange and introduce Japanese culture around the world. He has published many books about origami.

編集——宮下　真（オフィス M2）
アートディレクション——有山達也
デザイン——池田千草、中島美佳（アリヤマデザインストア）
撮影——石川美香
千代紙スタイリング——田中美和子
作品制作・折り図作成——湯浅信江
英訳—— Sarah McNally
協力——伊澤悠紀子
折り図トレース——株式会社ファクトリー・ウォーター

千代紙・撮影協力——「ゆしまの小林」
　　　　　　　　　　お茶の水・おりがみ会館
　　　　　　　　　　URL　http://www.origamikaikan.co.jp/

参考文献————『日本の文様』（小林一夫著・日本ヴォーグ社）
　　　　　　　『日本・中国の文様事典』（視覚デザイン研究所）
　　　　　　　『折形の礼法　暮らしに息づく和紙の美学』（山根章弘著・大和書房）
　　　　　　　『折形レッスン　美しい日本の包み方』（山根一城著・文化出版局）

英訳付き　包む折り紙帖

監修者　小林一夫
発行者　池田士文
印刷所　図書印刷株式会社
製本所　図書印刷株式会社
発行所　株式会社池田書店
　　　　東京都新宿区弁天町43番地（〒162-0851）
　　　　☎ 03-3267-6821（代）／振替 00120-9-60072
　　　　落丁、乱丁はお取り替えいたします。

©K. K. Ikeda Shoten 2008, Printed in Japan
ISBN978-4-262-15271-4